BRAZILIAN
JIU-JITSU
ADVANCED
TECHNIQUES

Also by Fabio Gurgel

BRAZILIAN JIU-JITSU / Basic Techniques

BRAZILIAN
JIU-JITSU
ADVANCED
TECHNIQUES

Fabio Duca Gurgel do Amaral
Eight-time World Champion

BLUE SNAKE BOOKS
BERKELEY, CALIFORNIA

Dekel Publishing House

Dekel Publishing House
P.O. Box 45094; Tel Aviv 61450, Israel
www.dekelpublishing.com
ISBN 978-965-7178-12-6

Original Brazilian edition by **Axcel Books**
Published in North America by **Blue Snake Books/Frog, Ltd.**

Blue Snake Books/Frog, Ltd. books are distributed by North Atlantic Books
P.O. Box 12327, Berkeley, California 94712, USA

Chief Editor: Ricardo Reinprecht
Co-Editor: Alexandre Esteves
Photography: Alexandre Vidal
Back Cover Photography: André Schiliró
English Translati
English Project I
Book and Cover

Production Editor: Gisella Narcisi
Original Cover & Design: Ingo Bertelli
Opponents in photos: Leonardo Vieira & Marcelo Garcia
Photography Editor: Carlos Alberto Sá Ferreira
Portuguese **Proofreader:** Alberto Garcia
English-language **Editor:** Efrat Ashkenazi
Technical **Advisor:** Branimir Tudjan

PLEASE NOT... ...ok disclaim any liabilities
for loss in co... ...s, exercises, and advice
contained her... ...y other harm, the reader
should consu... ...r any other martial arts,
movement, m... ...e instructions and advice
printed in this... ...titute for medical, mental,
or emotional... ...hcare provider.

Library of Congress Cataloging-in-Publication Data:
Gurgel, Fabio Duca do Amaral.
  Brazilian jiu-jitsu advanced techniques / by Fabio Gurgel.
      p. cm.
  "Original Brazilian edition by Axcel Books"--T.p. verso.
  Summary: "A practical guide building on its predecessor Brazilian jiu-jitsu basic techniques, Advanced techniques offers specific intermediate and advanced instruction as well as historical context"--Provided by publisher.
  ISBN-13: 978-1-58394-166-9 (trade paper)
  ISBN-10: 1-58394-166-5 (trade paper)
  1. Jiu-jitsu--Brazil. I. Title.
GV1114.G87 2007
796.815'2--dc22
                                        2007020646

1 2 3 4 5 6 7 8 9 Dekel Productions, Tel Aviv 12 11 10 09 08 07

Table of Contents

INTRODUCTION

I have been a Jiu-Jitsu practitioner since 1984 and a black belt for almost 16 years. Teaching classes and engaging in numerous competitions over the years enabled me to closely follow the development of our sport, which in Brazil has grown more in the last 15 years than through all its prior history. This growth did not bring benefits only to Jiu-Jitsu, however, for the sport has spread throughout the national territory, often reaching far from its worldwide center, Rio de Janeiro. This caused a serious problem: misinformed, low-quality teachers, a phenomenon that threatens Jiu-Jitsu's homogeneity – and homogeneity would be ideal for our sport.

With this in mind, I decided to produce a far-reaching manual that could help not only students wishing to learn new techniques, but also teachers interested in refreshing their knowledge, so as to improve the quality of their lessons and their students.

I have already written three books and released three videotape collections presenting my favorite techniques. The success they achieved made me realize that Jiu-Jitsu is overcoming its parochial nature and becoming unified as it grows and evolves more and more, no matter which academy or martial arts studio the teacher comes from. This has made me even prouder and spurred me to write yet another book – this two-volume manual of Brazilian Jiu-Jitsu in English.

When I decided to engage in this work, I did so because I believed, as of course I still do, that my dream would be brought closer, and that one more step in this long journey would be taken — a journey which I am certain I am not making alone, for each teacher, each white-belt student, each lover of our art makes their contribution every day, bringing us closer to our dream.

I believe in Jiu-Jitsu as a way of life, and I think that enthusiasts worldwide will recognize this art, originally part of the Brazilian culture and now more than ever belonging to the entire world. This is the highest recognition and the greatest contribution Jiu-Jitsu can make to society. I know the path is long and arduous, but I view Jiu-Jitsu practitioners no longer as a family, but as an army – a peaceful one, of course, because the negative image that some people tried to attribute to us in the past has long disappeared. We will be strong enough to prove, by word and by deed, that our sport is composed of serious-minded people and a body of knowledge with the potential for improving the human essence and instilling self-assurance, humility, and equilibrium, three elements that can help make humans better beings.

Fabio Duca Gurgel do Amaral
São Paulo, Brazil
July 2007

HISTORY

Ever since I started practicing Jiu-Jitsu, I have been hearing the same tale about the origin of our fighting technique, a tale which, though many may already know it, still cannot be omitted from a book such as this. However, in addition to telling this tale, I also feel I cannot overlook the moment when the Gracie family first encountered Jiu-Jitsu.

More than 2,500 years ago, the first self-defense technique dispensing of the use of weapons was created by man: in that moment Jiu-Jitsu was born, fashioned by Buddhist monks, individuals who were physically weak and constantly targeted for attack during their pilgrimages. Inspired by the movements of animals in the wild, these monks developed levers, self-defense techniques, and having mastered them, were no longer molested during their travels. The Buddhist monks introduced their techniques in China, the first country to have contact with the new art. Before long, Jiu-Jitsu reached the Land of the Rising Sun, which was soon to be the cradle of all martial arts.

In those feudal times, Japanese lords and noblemen employed the Samurai for their protection. The Samurai were splendid warriors, who chose Jiu-Jitsu as their hand-to-hand fighting and defense technique.

This tale should be known in order that the philosophy of our fight can be better understood, for the Samurai fought to defend their masters, and only death could hold them back.

After this phase of history, and with the advent of the industrial revolution, Japanese ports were opened to the West. Enormous curiosity arose about Oriental culture - and, of course, also about the secrets of the martial arts, which were already the subject of extensive discussion in the West.

At this point, the Japanese were concerned with preserving their culture, as well as their knowledge of weapons and war techniques. Jiu-Jitsu became fragmented, and several arts, such as Karate, Judo and Aikido, among other techniques, thus began to be developed and exported and eventually became great fighting styles in their own right. Jiu-Jitsu, however, was preserved by the Japanese emperor, who decreed that its teaching outside Japan would be a crime against the Japanese nation.

During the years of World War I, many Japanese emigrated to the West, and a large number of them came to Brazil. Belém do Pará, in the state of Pará, in the northern part of Brazil, was the city in which Count Maeda Koma, the Japanese champion at the time, chose to make his home. Belém do Pará was also the place of residence of Gastão Gracie and his sons: Carlos, George, Osvaldo, Gastão and

Hélio. An influential man, the Gracie patriarch soon made the acquaintance of the count, helping him in the new city and winning his friendship.

Feeling grateful towards his friend, the count decided to teach, on condition of secrecy, the most perfect form of fighting to Gastão's eldest son, Carlos. Jiu-Jitsu soon captured the interest of the very talented Carlos, who within a short time perfectly mastered all the techniques. He soon began to teach his brothers. It was the inception of a clan that would dominate first the realm of Brazilian martial arts and, shortly thereafter, that of the whole world. Hélio Gracie has a history of his own. The greatest genius of our sport developed new techniques, so efficient that they became known as simply "perfect."

At the outset, however, Hélio had medical limitations that prevented him from engaging in sports. He could not endure strenuous physical activities, and fainted whenever he tried. However, he watched every one of his brothers' lessons, and greatly wished to do as they did. One day his elder brother was late for class, and from then on Hélio became a "teacher," for he knew the entire program perfectly, just from watching. Thus the most perfect fighter of all time was born.

Hélio, besides treading the arduous path of proving Jiu-Jitsu's superiority to all other fighting styles and engaging in Ultimate Fighting all over the country, was able to keep the whole family under his command, training his people so that Jiu-Jitsu would never be forgotten. And he succeeded in doing so: Hélio stopped fighting at the age of 45, making way for the family's second phenomenon, Carlson Gracie*, who, more than anyone else, engaged in Ultimate Fighting without ever knowing defeat, trained excellent students, and wrote many important pages in the history of Jiu-Jitsu. However, while Carlson was breaking the rings apart, Hélio was already preparing his successor. Rolls Gracie earned his black belt at the age of 16, and from that time on, no one ever heard about his guard being broken.

Rolls was a complete fighter, perfect when standing, and also a practitioner of wrestling. A real 'animal' when in his kimono: quick, flexible, lethal - the greatest finisher in the history of his family. He was, beyond doubt, the third phenomenon of Jiu-Jitsu.

The story of Rolls was told to me by my master Romero Cavalcanti, the "Jacaré." Romero Cavalcanti had trained with Rolls until his death in 1982, at age 32, in a hang-gliding accident, and was the last black belt he graduated. After his passing came the fourth and current Jiu-Jitsu phenomenon: Rickson Gracie, who needs no introduction and who, fortunately for Jiu-Jitsu, will be with us for a long time.

Of course, Jiu-Jitsu does not consist exclusively of Gracies. Each of us is a part of the wonderful history I have just related, for lines such as that of Rolls, who taught "Jacaré," who taught me, who teaches my students, will continue to expand

* Grandmaster Carlson Gracie died in Chicago on February 1st, 2006, at the age of 72.

further and further. This endless movement takes our sport to such achievements as those seen today in the United States and many other countries, where people want to discover why the Brazilian fighters are so much better in Jiu-Jitsu. The answer is: because it is part of our culture and because we respect our history and that of Jiu-Jitsu.

1

SELF-DEFENSE

Perhaps the most important segment of Jiu-Jitsu, the real foundation of everything else but often overlooked by many, is personal defense. It occurs when the student learns to defend himself and begins the process of becoming a complete fighter capable of going up against any combatant of whatever modality. Do not delude yourself into believing that learning your guard well will save you from a real combat situation: personal defense must be learned and trained as much as, or more than, the competition part. It will be the source of all your self-confidence, and will give you the bearing of a great fighter.

• JAB DEFENSE

In guard position, make sure your
front hand (the left hand in the
picture) corresponds to the front foot,
so that you may be able to defend
yourself from any kind of attack.

When the opponent throws his jabs,
do not create a rearward pendulum
because this will allow him to
proceed in a sequence of strikes.
Do the opposite: project your body
forward, deflecting the blow with
the hand close to your face and
simultaneously taking a step forward
with your front leg.

After that, take another outward step
off your opponent's body, grabbing
hold of his waist and placing your
head on the back of his shoulder
(which will prevent him from striking
you with his elbow).

4 Take a step with your left leg, so as to place it parallel to the other leg and, on your opponent's back, move your hip to his rear, creating the lever that will enable you to lift him off the ground.

5 Perform a hip throw without releasing the hands.

6 Follow the throw to the end, so that your opponent falls with his chest facing the ground.

Mount his back and finish with a rear naked choke.

• DEFENSE FROM TECHNICAL CHOKE

A very common situation is that of
this choke, which is called technical
because, unlike others, it is truly
efficient as a form of choke.

First, grab hold of the hand around your neck, hugging the opponent over the shoulder with your other arm, thus partly relieving the pressure of the choke.

Take a step towards the side opposite your head, that is, the same side as the arm hugging the opponent's shoulder.

4

Free your hand from the opponent's wrist and place it between his legs. Note that the hand is placed with its back on the leg, in order to perform the movement: do not try to apply excessive force with this hand.

5

Use your hip to lift your opponent off the ground, slipping your arm between his legs so as to sustain his weight.

Complete the throw and place your knee on your opponent's belly to dominate him.

6

• DEFENSE FROM A SLAP ON THE FACE

At a safe distance, the opponent prepares his attack. Just remain attentive and on the ready.

When the opponent attempts to strike you, take a step forward with the leg on the same side as his attacking hand, and block his biceps with your forearm. Place your hand in a hook-shape on his triceps, keeping him from moving back, which he will try to do in order to execute a new attack.

3 Take one step towards the side opposite his attack, hugging his back and protecting your head by keeping it close to your chest, reducing the distance and placing yourself out of range of all attacks.

Extend your leg behind the opponent's body, pulling him over it by forcing him back with the hand that is on his waist, and with the help of your head.

4

5 Complete the throw and get the opponent in side control.

• DEFENSE FROM A FORWARD KICK

Stand motionless before your opponent, facing him. This attack is usually executed by surprise.

When the attack begins, turn your torso while holding your extended arm close to your body, so as to deflect the kick.

3 Put your other arm around the opponent's leg, grabbing it from the underside, taking a step forward and hugging his back with the arm that you used to deflect the kick.

With the leg on the same side as the arm around your opponent's body, do **4** a sweep on the inside of the leg that is on the ground.

5 Throw your opponent to the ground.

Remain standing until the movement is over, and be ready for a guard pass.

• TURNAROUND CHOKE

Once you are caught in a choke, there are a few things you must do. First, you should look towards your opponent's body, so as to neutralize any kind of choke. Second, protect your face from any attempt he may make to punch you.

This done, begin your defense by taking one step forward and pressing your knees against each other. At the same time, place your hand (with the palm turned up) on the back of your opponent's knee.

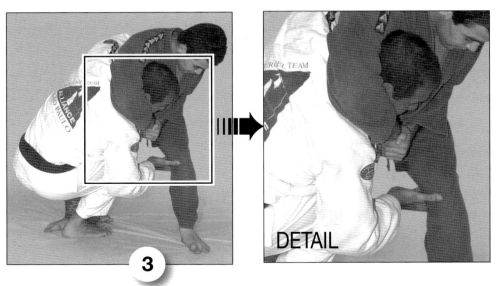

DETAIL

3

Begin the movement by turning your body, so as to crouch between your aggressor's legs; use the hand that is on his waist to pull him along with your movement.

4

Sit on the floor and continue your movement in the same direction, so as to roll over the shoulder (in this case, the left one).

Keep your hand behind your opponent's knee and, while still rolling, start passing your leg over his legs.

This way, you will end up mounted, with one leg standing and both hands on the ground, so as to keep your balance as well as to be in a control position.

Press your wrist bone behind your opponent's ear and push your body up and forward, thus breaking the choke hold.

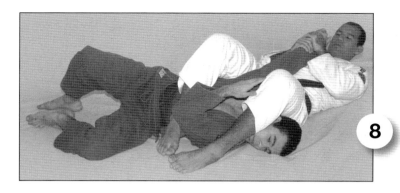

8 Once you have freed your arm, finish with an armlock.

• TWO-LAPEL GRAB

The opponent grabs hold of both your lapels, intending to shake you back and forth.

1

2 When he pulls you forward, take advantage of his outstretched arms. Use the extra space to put your arms in and extend them upward.

3 Put your arms over and around those of your opponent, and grab your own wrist with your other hand, so that your opponent will not be able to pull his arms back. Your head should be touching his shoulder.

Take a step towards the same side as your head, and extend the opposite leg just in front of your opponent's body, pulling him forward and turning his torso.

4

5 Your opponent's arms being now immobilized, he will be forced to roll, and you should follow his movement.

Assume a mounting position at the end of the roll, and release the hands so as to regain balance.

• DOUBLE NELSON

The opponent dominates you in double nelson style.

Immediately put your hands on your forehead and push your head back, so as to keep your chin from touching your chest, which would make the defense much more difficult.

3 Put both your hands together just in front of your belly, and put your arms around those of the opponent, preferably from behind his elbows.

Take a step to the rear of your opponent. Your leg must pass just behind your supporting leg and in front of your opponent's leg. **4**

5 Kneel down on your front leg, in the middle of your opponent's leg, and begin a roll between his legs.

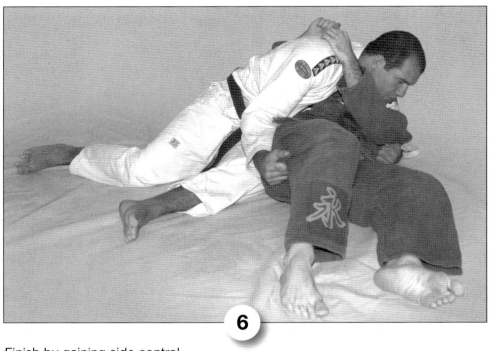

6

Finish by gaining side control.

2

PASSING THE GUARD

This chapter, intended to discuss guard passes, is slightly complex, for, like everything about Jiu-Jitsu, you depend on your opponent's reactions to properly apply the correct technique at any given moment. Thus, there is no single best guard pass; there is just the best time for each of them to be used. Still, even when you choose the right time, you must rely on your opponent's defense. That is where the combinations come in, which are, in truth, the real secret about passing the guard. Knowing how to use variations is a key factor for a successful pass. You should, therefore, exercise each technique separately, and start training the variations between them only after you have mastered each one individually. You will thus open a broad range of possibilities, developing your capacity to create indefensible situations. Another indispensable factor is rhythm: once you achieve a good pass position, you must keep your opponent in permanent peril, blocking any attempt to attack or sweep. This, too, will depend on your variations, because if you have a new form of attack for each defense attempted by your opponent, you will be sure to accomplish your objective.

• PASSING THE GUARD WITH LEG CRUSH

Start with your opponent defending his guard, holding up your elbow with the knee and controlling both your sleeves.

Put your chin outside your opponent's knee. As you press your chin down, use the opposite hand to help lower the leg he was holding against you towards the side.

Then, with your other hand, dominate the opponent's lower leg, at thigh height; pay close attention because your hand must not pass between his legs, and your elbow must be pressed against his thigh. Control his sleeve with your other hand.

Raise both knees from the ground and put your head against your opponent's belly: this will help you distribute your weight, resulting in a better dominance.

4

DETAIL

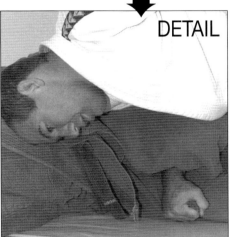

The detail shows how you should position your hand.

5

Put your knee closer to your opponent's hip and take your head off his belly, thus keeping him from going into a guard stance.

6

Hold him in side control and pass the guard!

• PASSING THE GUARD WITH KNEE CROSS

Start on your opponent's open guard, with one hand on one of his lapels and the other as high as his knee. Make sure your balance is good and your weight is well distributed.

Placing your hand at the height of your opponent's knee, lower it towards the ground while taking a step forward with the leg on the same side. This is done while crossing the knee on the same side as the hand, which is on the opponent's lapel over the leg that you have just put down.

Control the sleeve and kick the leg of the knee that was crossed forward. Keep your hand on the opponent's collar and force your elbow down, so as to block his hip escape movement.

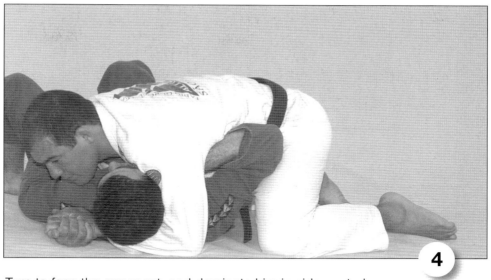

Turn to face the opponent, and dominate him in side control.

• PASSING THE GUARD WITH HANDS ON SHINBONE

Start in open guard, with your opponent controlling the position with one foot on the biceps and the other on the groin.

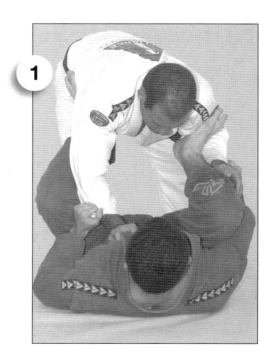

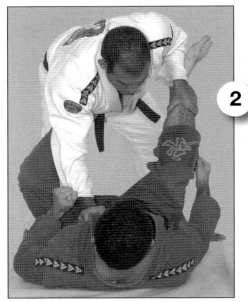

The hand on the same side as the biceps must grab hold of your opponent's shin on the same side. To do this, you need to turn your hand, which is behind his leg on your biceps, and only then proceed to dominate his shin. Keep the other hand on your opponent's collar.

Press down on his shin and take a step forward, so as to keep the opponent's leg trapped between your legs. Pay attention to weight distribution: you should not lean either forwards or backwards during this movement.

With the leg that remained between your opponent's legs, step back and then forward, around and out of your opponent's legs. Only then will you release the shin.

Grab your opponent's sleeve and press your knee over his belly, at the same time dominating the guard pass.

• PASSING THE GUARD WITH HANDS ON HIPS

After opening guard, simultaneously place both hands under your opponent's legs.

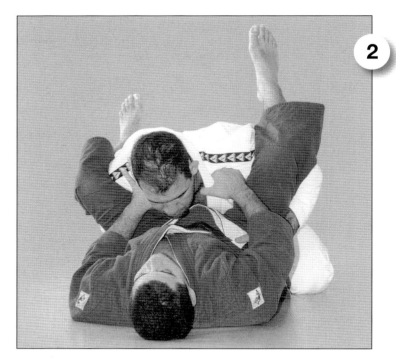

2 Kneel down on both legs and pull your opponent's hips towards you.

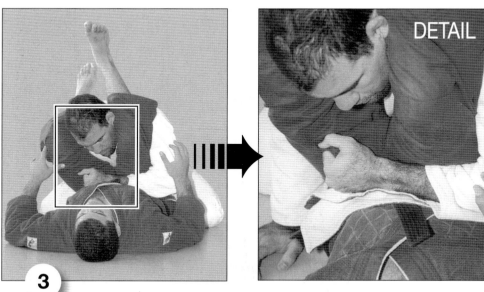

DETAIL

3

Normally, you cannot just grab your opponent's collar in order to flip him over and pass the guard. When this is the case, you should grab his trousers with the hand opposite his hips, with your forearm alongside it (see detail).

Stretch your leg back, taking both feet from the ground and leaning with all your weight over your opponent's hips, pressing him down with your elbow.

Lower your hips, pressing your navel area down, and keep hold of his trousers, so as to prevent hip escape.

Pass the guard, dominating the opponent's shoulders from under his arms and placing your chest over his.

• PASSING THE HALF-GUARD WITH SHIN ON THIGH

Secure your
opponent in
a half-guard,
noting the
position of his
pinned leg. Your
foot must be
close to his hip.

Raise your
hips and place
your knee
over his belly,
putting your
shin against his
thigh.

Sit on the
ground again
and position
your hand, so
as to push your
opponent's
knee.

Pull your leg out from between your opponent's legs. The shin you are holding against his thigh will make a perfect lever for you to accomplish this easily.

Turn your torso and pass the guard.

• PASSING THE GUARD WITH A STAR

Start on open guard, grabbing your opponent's collar at the same side as his foot that is on your groin.

Take advantage of the movement in which he tries to push you away with his foot, in order to drive your head towards his belly. Your other hand should be on the floor as a support.

Throw your legs upwards in a star movement, and keep your body as straight as possible, so as to escape more easily from his foot on your groin.

Start turning your hips in the air, so that your approach is well-balanced.

Put both feet on the ground at the same time, and keep your head on his belly.

Move to your opponent's side and get him in side control.

• PASSING THE GUARD WITH A HOOK HUGGING THE BACK

This pass begins when your opponent tries to enter on guard with hooks on the inside.

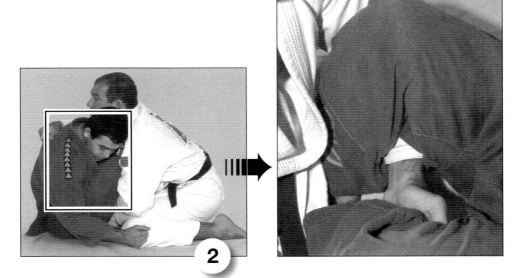

Grab the back part of his kimono with the hand on the same side as your head. Grab the leg on the same side by passing your other hand under the opponent's other leg, as shown in the detail. Keep sitting on your heels and do not let yourself lean forward.

3

Switch legs by falling towards the same side as the hand that is grabbing his back. Make sure not to release the leg grab until the end of the movement. Press your head on your opponent's chest.

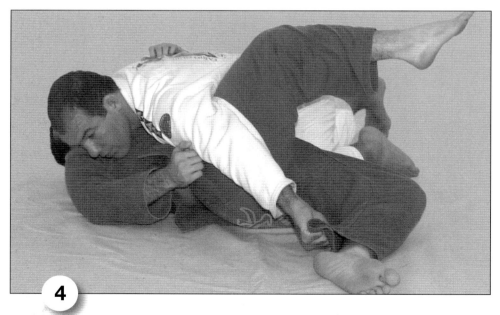

4

Turn to face him. Do not release his leg. Hug his head and dominate him in side control.

SWEEPS

This chapter discusses sweeps. Undoubtedly, the sweep is the most evolving technique of Jiu-Jitsu competition nowadays, and also one of the most complex to learn and train. The principle of sweeps is one of balance: anyone who is only partially on the ground is already off balance. Every situation thus has its own particular sweep, together with the proper lever effect that we should seek in order to execute a more precise movement. Like everything about Jiu-Jitsu, we will be facing an opponent who will try to do exactly the opposite of what we want, and that is why there are sweep combinations. If, for instance, we attempt a sweep in which our opponent is to be thrown forward, he will naturally try to put his weight back in order to defend himself. It is precisely then that we bring in the combination, using a sweep that will throw him in whatever direction his weight can help us most. If we have a good repertoire of sweeps, every time our opponent is even slightly off balance we will have an opportunity to switch between sweeps until one of them proves successful. Training these techniques is very important, for it often occurs that a little imbalance will not only lead to a sweep, but to a finishing as well.

• HOOK SWEEP

Begin in position with both feet on the inner side of your opponent's legs, sitting with your back off the ground.

Grab his belt by putting your hand under his arm that is opposite your head. Put the other hand on your opponent's knee and pull it towards the underside of his body, getting as close as possible.

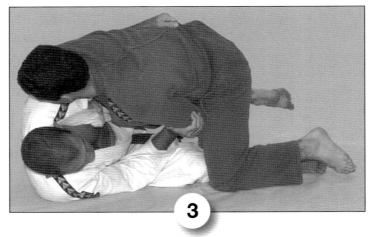

Start the movement by pulling the opponent's belt towards you, pushing the elbow inwards with the hand that was on his knee and raising the hook of the opposite side. Make sure you are lying on your shoulder at this moment.

4 Proceed with your movement until the end of the hook.

When you are almost in a mount position, you will notice that your foot is stuck in a half-guard.

5

6 To rectify this, take advantage of your arm's current position and cross over the knee to the other side, passing the guard and assuming side control.

• SWEEP WITH CROSSED HOOKS

Begin in position with both feet on the inner side of your opponent's legs, sitting with your back off the ground.

Begin the hook sweep. Notice that in order to avoid you, your opponent moves his leg so as to create a new support.

Release the arm and grab hold of the leg on which your opponent is supporting himself; keep the hand on the belt tightly closed.

4

Pull the leg and move your hip inward so as to stand sideways relative to your opponent. This is the time to place the second hook. Keep in mind that the second hook must always be put over the first hook, which was already in position since the beginning.

5

Watch how the hooks are placed from a different angle. Also, pay attention to the knee of the second hook: it must be turned outward. Now move the hand grasping the belt and grab hold of the sleeve of the arm that the opponent is using for support next to your legs.

Grab hold of his sleeve and extend both legs, so as to begin moving into a sitting position. Your opponent will be suspended in the air, completely unbalanced.

6

7 Finish by moving on top of your opponent and putting your knee on his belly.

• THRUSTING IN TO SIDE CONTROL

This sweep must be used when your opponent tries to pass guard placing one hand inside your legs, as shown in the picture. Sit down and slide your hand over your opponent's shoulder and down to his armpit. **1**

2

Wait for your opponent's guard pass before you begin yours. Put your hand on the floor, so that it may help your hip escape. Be very careful: the arm on the opponent's armpit must be exactly as in the picture, in front of his face.

Slide your hip out with a single movement, using the hand on the armpit to draw your opponent towards an open space.

Immediately move the hand that was on the ground for support to your opponent's belt, so as to prevent him from raising his head and blocking the sweep. While doing so, put the hand that had been on his armpit around his leg.

Pull the leg and the belt and project your body forward, standing on your knees and completing the sweep.

• HOOK AND THROW SWEEP

Start in the same position as the
previous sweeps.

Your opponent places his leg
between yours, removing your foot
from his groin and breaking your
dominant position.

Immediately
make a hook
behind his leg
to keep him
under control.

Place the foot that was on your opponent's biceps as high as his belt, pulling him over you with both arms. Your knees must be hidden and close to your chest.

4

Extend both legs, lifting your opponent off the ground.

5

6

Roll back and finish in mount position.

• CROSSED ARM SWEEP

Start in a sitting position, facing the opponent. Dominate the arm with the hand on the opposite side. With your other hand, grab hold of your opponent's kimono, on his shoulder.

Escape with your hip towards the same side as the dominated arm, pulling the arm so as to force your opponent to put his hand on the ground for support.

Quickly grab his belt, while moving your hips even further away. Put your elbow on the floor, as if you were moving towards your opponent's rear.

Attempting to protect his back, your opponent will be vulnerable to a sweep. Place your arm under his armpit and move your hips back, with your lower back remaining on the ground. Make sure the arm that was dominated when the movement began is caught between your body and that of your opponent, so as to keep him from freeing this arm. Apply pressure with the elbow of the arm on the same side as the hand on his belt.

Do a hook sweep, sliding your hip towards the side opposite to where the movement began.

Finish in a mount position.

• FEET-ON-BICEPS SWEEP

Start in an open guard with your opponent on his knees. Control both sleeves.

1

2

Slide your hip and put your foot on his biceps of the same side. Keep the other foot on the opponent's groin, and control both sleeves.

Begin the sweep by stretching the leg of the same side as the biceps and, while in a sitting position, put your elbow on the ground, letting the other leg fall outside your opponent's body.

3

This leg, which is on the outside, must sweep your opponent's supporting knee by executing a lateral movement and also rotating your body in order to cause your opponent to be swept diagonally.

4

5

Only when the movement is completed should you remove your feet from his biceps and go into a mount position.

• SPIDER SWEEP

Start with
the same
domination
as seen in the
**Hook and
Throw Sweep**
(Page 42).

Lie on your hip
so as to reach
the opponent's
heel with the
hand that
was on his
collar. The leg
that was on
his biceps is
stretched on the
ground between
his legs.

Using both hands, pull the opponent's leg out from under him until your leg meets his, causing him to fall back. You must touch his heel with the part of your leg that is just above the sinew. The foot that is on his groin makes the opposite movement, pushing the hips.

Kneel down and get hold of your opponent in a half-guard.

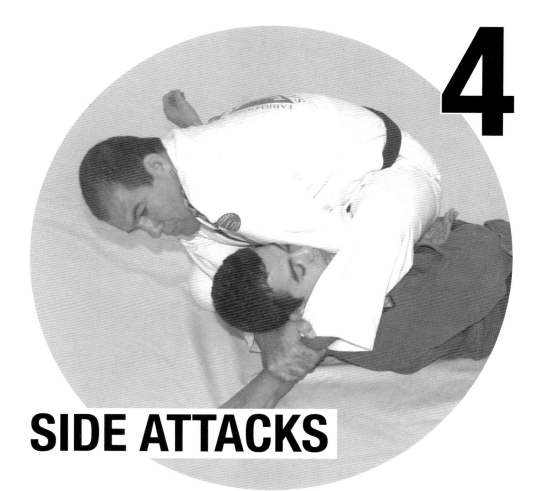

SIDE ATTACKS

The attacks for the side control position are highly diversified. This is also a position of extreme control. The fear of losing position, however, often causes people not to risk attack, and they limit themselves to pinning down their opponents, which results in a game with only a few offensives. I believe in a bold Jiu-Jitsu, which looks for a finish in any position, especially in one so rich in attacks. You need only to keep some details in mind: distribute your weight so as to keep your body relaxed at all times, for tension makes it more susceptible to inversions and, obviously, makes you waste too much energy. Almost all attacks in this position, when concerned with defense, can be easily replaced by others. With a little practice, you can begin creating endless finishing situations starting from any move, which means your opponent will find it very difficult to defend himself. Remember: the attacks must be tight, so as to leave no room for escape (unless such space is created for your own benefit). Do as the chess player does, and close off all defense options until you achieve checkmate.

• COLLAR CHOKE

Start in side control position with one hand around the opponent's head and the other hand free to prepare the collar attack. Make sure your knee is close to your opponent's hip, so as to keep him from regaining his guard.

Pull the collar from underneath your opponent's elbow and grab it with the hand that is around his head; pass the collar from one hand to another, grabbing it as tightly as you can.

Now that the collar is in your grasp, pull it as hard as you can; it will usually get as far as the nape of your opponent's neck.

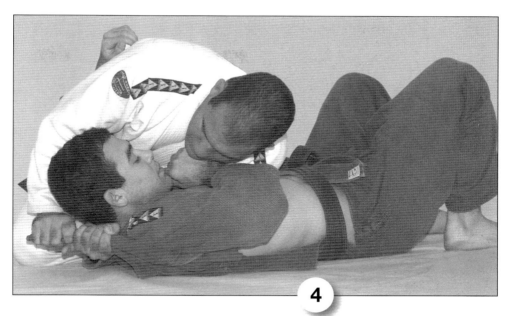

4

Change hands again. Now you must be completely attentive in order not to lose control. Put your elbow over your opponent's belly and grab his collar at a point as close as possible to the place where you are already holding it.

5

The attack is fully prepared, and now you just need to finish it. To do so put your other hand over your opponent's shoulder and as close as possible to your first hand on the same lapel. Pull it towards your chest, raising your opponent's back from the ground and tightening the choke.

• WRAPPED ARM CHOKE

Begin the attack
in the north/
south position.

Your opponent makes the mistake of putting his arms around your back. Take
advantage of this situation by wrapping your arm around his and grabbing his
collar with the palm of your hand turned up.

Move to the side by changing guard and pulling up the collar.

Grab the other lapel with your thumb on the outside.

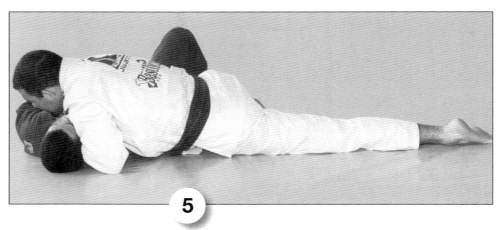

Turn so as to face your opponent, completely extending your leg and placing your elbow and hips on the ground. Slide your elbow up and against his neck, finishing the choke.

• GUILLOTINE CHOKE

Begin in side
control, opening
the opponent's
collar and
putting your arm
around the back
of his neck.

Take advantage
of his open
collar and put
your other
hand in, with
palm open,
and move
it forcefully
towards your
other hand.

The detail
shows the hand
movement.

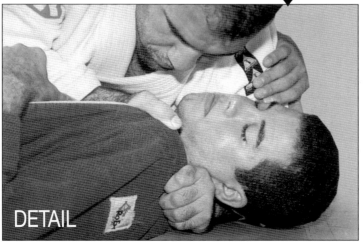

DETAIL

Begin turning
towards the
north/south
direction,
placing your
elbows very
close together
and pressing
your head
against your
opponent's
chest.

Put the inside
of your knee
against your
opponent's face,
to keep him
from escaping,
and tighten
the choke by
drawing your
hands towards
you as if trying
to rip his kimono
apart.

• KATAGATAME

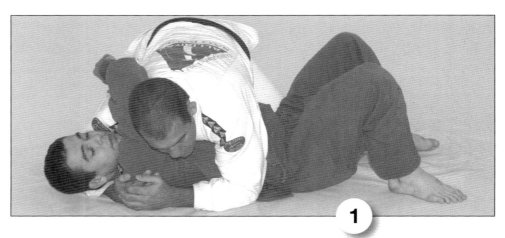

Start in side control, but pay attention to your opponent's arm, which is placed
over your shoulder.

Propel your head diagonally forward, so as to keep your opponent from removing his arm. Grab hold of his biceps to tighten the position.

Cross your knee over the opponent's belly, so as to keep him from regaining half guard, which would make your attack more difficult. Put all your weight on his head.

Once you get to the other side, kick the leg you had crossed over your opponent's belly well forward, so as to leave your legs spread, resembling the hands of a clock.

Execute
the choke
by pressing
down with the
shoulder that
is over your
opponent's
neck. Make
sure the
movement is
one leading not
to a cervical
lock, but to a
choke.

• KIMURA AND NUTCRACKER

Start with the
arm already
twisted as
in inverted
domination.

In attempting
to free his arm,
your opponent
will give you
the opportunity
for a Kimura
lock. Take
advantage of
this opportunity
immediately.

3

However, the opponent may be too strong and might hold back the arm, so as to make the lock too difficult. If that is the case, slide your leg under your opponent's head. Use the leg on the same side as the arm you are attacking.

Lie down on your side and cross the other leg over your opponent's neck, locking the legs so as to leave his neck between them, and then tighten the choke.

4

• ARMLOCK WITH KNEES TOUCHING

Start in side control position.

1

Put your knee under your opponent's elbow and press down with your shoulder over his face.

Leave the dominating position and put your other knee over your opponent's shoulder, as if you were squeezing it between your legs.

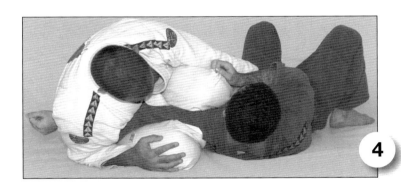

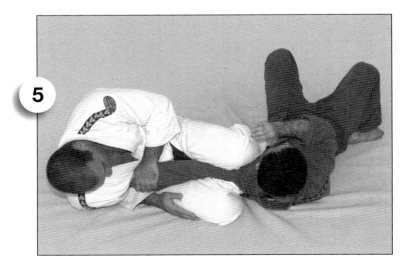

Lie on your side with knees nearly touching, and be sure to maintain pressure.

Stretch your body back to finish the armlock, and keep the opponent's wrist under your armpit so as to increase the lever effect. This lock must be attempted very quickly, and always by surprise.

• TRIANGLE

Start in side
control position,
but make sure
your knee is
very close to
your opponent's
head, keeping
his elbow on
the outer side of
your hip.

Push his leg
with your hand
and threaten to
put your knee
on his belly.

In attempting
to defend
himself, your
opponent will
push your knee.
That is when
you should
dominate his
wrist by pushing
it against his
belly. Then take
a back step.

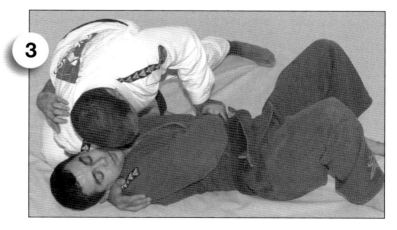

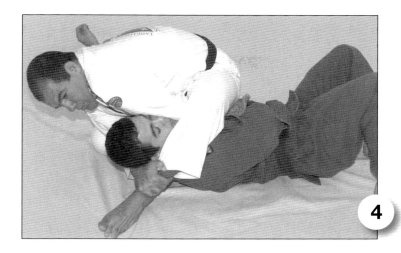

Mount your opponent's arm by placing your leg straight over his shoulder. Grab your shin with the other hand.

4

Roll over to the same side as the leg that is twisted around the opponent's head, and put the other foot on his groin to fine-tune the position and help you lock the triangle.

5

6

Close the triangle, pull the head back and finish it. Make sure to position your arm diagonally, so as to further enhance your attack.

MOUNTED ATTACKS

We now arrive at Jiu-Jitsu's supreme position, one of extreme superiority and total domination but also full of details, for imbalance is constant here, and you must know how to use it to your advantage. Imbalance will often bring you benefits, but you need to train very hard in order to find your own point of balance and comfort when mounted. Choking is an excellent starting point for attacks in this position, because it is sufficient to put one hand on your opponent's collar for him to begin to worry about being choked, and it is precisely through his worries that you can achieve a better position. It is essential not to remain sitting over your opponent's belly because this is his main point, from which he could create a lever in order to displace your weight and get out of his predicament. Therefore, you must put your knees forward in order to sit on your own heels, which also opens the possibility of attacking the arm, in addition to choking.

• HAND-ON-ARMPIT ARMLOCK

Start in a mount position with both hands on the floor.

In attempting to escape, your opponent will make a bridge by pushing with both hands under your armpits. His body will be projected forward. The hand on the same side as the arm that will be attacked should be put on the ground, at some distance from your body.

Slide your knee on the same side as the arm that will be attacked, leaving it in the same direction as your opponent's head.

4 Lie back, hugging the opponent's arm and raising his knee. It is not necessary to pass the leg over his head, because this would create enough space for your opponent to move out, and the attack would become much slower.

5

Finish in an armlock by grabbing hold of the aggressor's wrist and keeping your knees close together.

• DOUBLE ATTACK WRISTLOCK

Start by placing one hand deep in your opponent's collar.

1

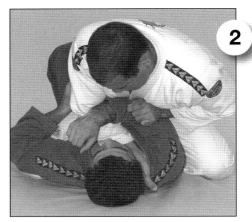

Push his arm inward, so as to immobilize his elbow with your torso.

Put your knee forward along the same line as your opponent's head, and raise your other leg slightly.

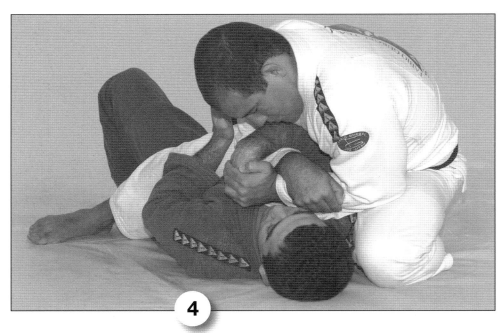

When you notice that your opponent's hand is free, grab the back of his hand, and with your hand that was holding his collar, grab hold of your own wrist, pressing the hand towards your belly and finishing the wristlock.

• ARMLOCK WITH ARM EXCHANGE

Start in a mounted double attack position.

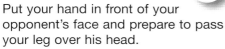

Put your hand in front of your opponent's face and prepare to pass your leg over his head.

When you have done so, your opponent chooses to defend his arm by grasping one with the other. At this moment, put the hand that is around his arm on your own collar and extend the other arm behind you, so as to remain in a sitting position.

Change the attack side. To do so, kneel down on the leg that was over your opponent's belly on the other side. Push yourself forward with the hand you are using to keep yourself in a sitting position. The other leg must be bent so that your foot is aligned with your head, because this way both arms will be immobilized.

Press your knees together, so as to keep the opponent from freeing his arms. Remove the hand that was between them and use it to grab the wrist of the arm that is to be attacked.

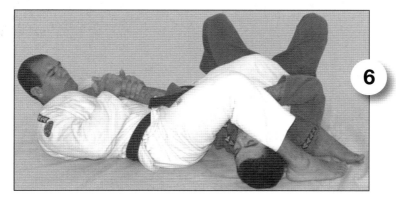

Pass your leg over his head and lie back towards the opposite side, finishing your opponent in an armlock.

• ARMLOCK WITH KNEES OVER CHEST

Start in a mounted position, hugging your opponent's head.

Realizing that your opponent's arm is over your back, project your body diagonally and get a tight hold of your own collar.

Put your head on the ground and stretch out your body as much as possible.

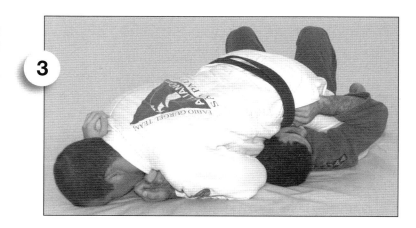

Put your hand on your opponent's head and cross your knee over his chest until it reaches the ground. The other leg must also be crossed. Put the foot of your other leg over your opponent's belly.

4

5

Keep your hips straight and apply pressure by pulling the arm towards your chest. Note that your arm is twisted around the opponent's arm as high as the elbow, resulting in a very tight armlock.

• SHOULDER BONE ARMLOCK

Again, start in a mounted double attack position.

1

Pass the leg over your opponent's face, attempting an armlock. Once it is defended, get in position by putting one hand on your own lapel and the other on the ground, extending your arm.

With the hand that was supporting you from behind, pull the elbow of the opposite arm towards your body.

With the leg that was over the opponent's belly in the previous step, press the arm as high as his triceps, forcing him to turn his body inward. When he does so, take the leg from his head so as to perform an easy hip escape, until your opponent is turned belly-down.

Hug the opponent's back, bend your leg backwards and start tightening the shoulder-bone lock by pressing your hip forward and your head towards the ground.

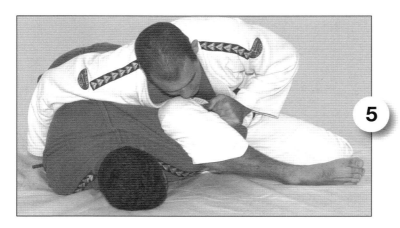

• SLEEVE CHOKE

Your opponent tries to escape your mount. He begins an elbow escape, turning his body to one side.

First, raise your leg by placing your heel very close to his stomach, while at the same time positioning the other knee so as to align it with your opponent's head.

The first hand works as a helper, stretching the lapel so that the hand that is moving behind his head can grab it firmly and deep inside.

The helping hand is then moved to the back of your opponent's neck, to provide support for the choke.

After placing the hand at the back of his neck and freeing it from under his arm, extend both arms and finish the choke.

• THUMB CHOKE

Start in mount position.

Put your first hand deep into the back of your opponent's collar, making sure to position your wrist correctly, for this will determine the success of your attack. Keeping your palm turned up, start to propel your weight towards the same side of the collar that you just grabbed.

Kneel down beside your opponent's shoulder, slightly extending your leg on the opposite side and leaning your chest against your opponent's elbow, thus creating the possibility of an arm attack.

Put in the second hand, with your thumb on the inside, your wrist straight and firm, and your palm facing down.

4

5

Move your head towards the ground on the same side as your other hand. Finish by opening your knees to improve your stance, and then drawing the choke against your chest.

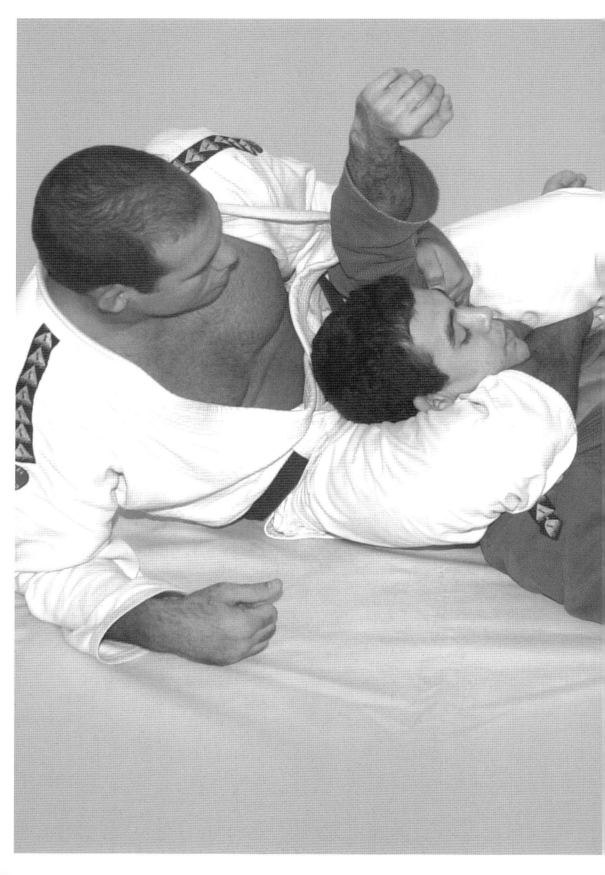

REAR ATTACKS

This position is extremely decisive. To wisely carry on the fight at this point is almost to define its results. For a rear attack to be successful, as is the case with all other positions, it is essential to know the possible ways of escape in order to predict your opponent's moves and intercept them. There are several ways to win the fight through rear attacks, but placing your hand on the collar over the opponent's shoulder is part of all of them, and this is precisely the first move you should try to make. After this, your next concern should be to hold your opponent in the position opposite the one that offers him a chance of escape. The next step would be to place your other hand correctly so as to create a second support, which will depend on the kind of attack you chose. Training for this technique must also be done separately: train just the rear attack, if your opponent escapes; restart if you are able to finish it; restart again and keep going. You will experience a fast progression and will be much more self-confident when attacking.

• ROLL AND HOOKS (REAR NAKED CHOKE)

Start in side control, with your opponent on all fours. Your knee must be on the ground between your opponent's knee and his elbow.

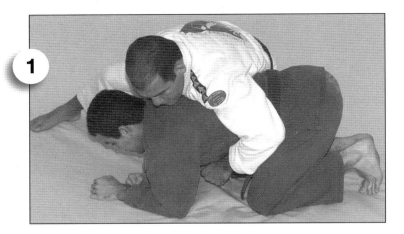

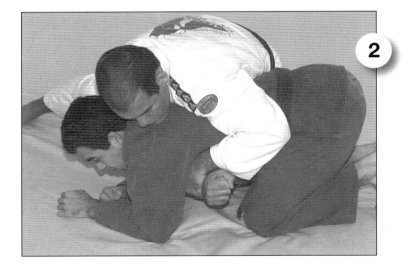

In the same position, hug your opponent's chest by putting one arm over the shoulder next to you and grabbing your own wrist with the other hand under your opponent's armpit, for a tight hold.

Press your shoulder over the nape of your opponent's neck, and put your back on the ground just in front of his head. Keep your hips raised.

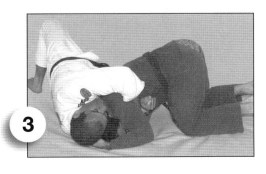

After putting your back on the ground, pull the opponent towards you and open your legs so as to position him between them.

4

When your opponent puts his feet on the ground, you need only to place the hooks that were waiting in position.

5

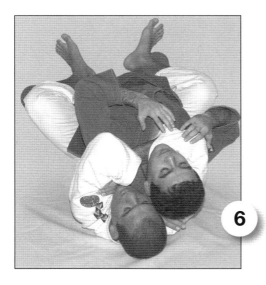

A possibility for rear naked choke usually arises when the opponent tries to defend himself from the hooks.

6

• CLOCK WITH ELBOW ON THE GROUND

Start in an
all-fours side
control position.

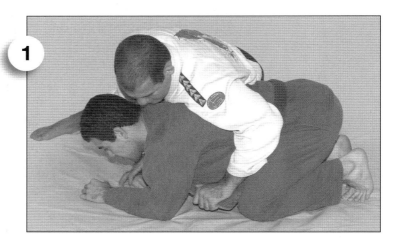

Put your hand
over your
opponent's
shoulder. Place
it as deep inside
his collar as you
can get.

After you have gained control of
the opponent's collar, he will expect
you to grab the wrist under his arm
to execute the traditional clock.
However, this would make room for
a variety of defenses. To avoid them,
place your elbow on the ground
close to the opponent's shoulder.
Your entire forearm should be on the
ground.

Kick the leg in front of you, with hips always off the ground, and tighten the collar upwards, finishing in a clock choke.

• OWN-COLLAR CHOKE

Start in an all-fours side control position.

Instead of attacking the opponent's collar, which is often inaccessible, hug him around the neck from over the shoulder of the opposite side.

3 Move to your opponent's other side by stepping over his back. Put your free hand on the ground in order to facilitate this move.

4

Put your knee on the ground and stretch the other leg away from your opponent's body, so that your weight will keep him from attempting any defense. At the same time, grab hold of your own collar and tighten the choke, as if you were contracting your biceps.

• REAR TRIANGLE

Start in position with your hooks already prepared. Your opponent will try to remove your hook with one of his hands.

1

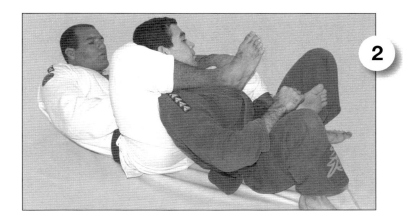

Before he dominates your heel, pass your leg over his shoulder on the same side as the arm he tried to defend.

This accomplished, put the foot of your other leg on the ground and slide your hips so that your leg that is over his shoulder will go around his neck, enabling you to lock the triangle.

Put your hand on the ground on one side and your foot on the other, so that you can raise your hip and tighten the choke. Your other hand must be holding his crossed knee, so as to keep your opponent from trying to turn himself belly-down, which would make the finish very difficult.

• ARMLOCK FROM HOOK DEFENSE

Start controlling
your opponent
while he is on
all fours.

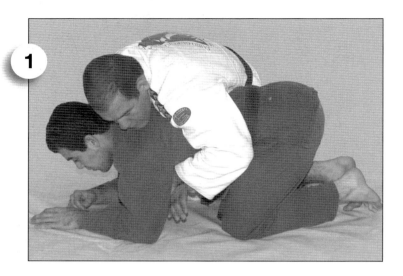

Roll back and
place the first
hook.

Start attacking your opponent's neck
by turning him to the other side in
order to make enough room to place
the second hook, from which in
this case your opponent will defend
himself by grabbing your foot.

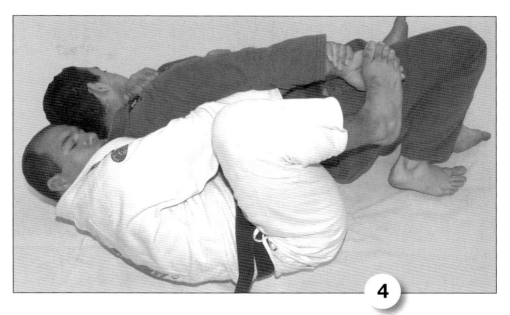

Change the hand that was attacking your opponent's collar and place it under his arm, grabbing his wrist.

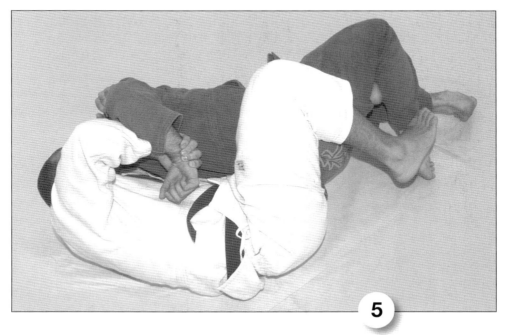

Ignore the hook and pull your opponent's hand backwards and upwards, finishing in an armlock.

• SOMERSAULT AND REAR GRAB

Starting in an all-fours position, hug your opponent's waist tightly. There must be no space between your arms and his body.

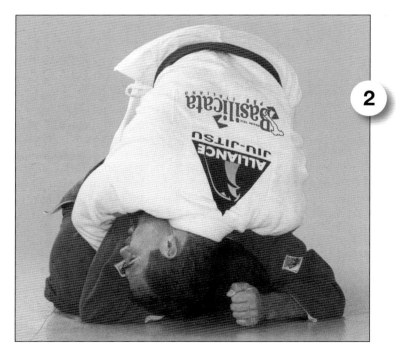

Lean your weight forward, placing your head beside your opponent's head, and facing outward.

Pull yourself up, stretching your legs upward and putting your head on the ground, creating a pendulum that will bring your opponent's body forward.

3

Put your back on the ground and pull your opponent towards you.

4

When the opponent falls in front of you, put both hooks in place and finish the position.

5

• SOMERSAULT AND HOOK

Start in the same position as in the previous attack. Cross-grab the lapels, bearing in mind the fact that the head must remain at the same side as the hand, which is deeper inside his collar.

Pull yourself up with legs outstretched, creating a pendulum to draw your opponent forward.

Put both feet on the ground and keep your hips high, adjusting both hands on your opponent's lapels. This will make him uncomfortable, and he will try to move back in order to free his head.

3

4 Somersault back over the same side of the head.

Set the hooks and grab hold of your opponent's back.

5

GUARD ATTACKS

Guard is one of the moments in Jiu-Jitsu that affords a big chance of finishing. Innumerable armlocks and chokes are possible in this position when it is closed, that is, when your legs are wrapped around your opponent's back. It is essential that you never let your opponent get into a position where he can stand and extend his leg; this would allow for a broad range of attack modes. Open guard, in turn, is much more unpredictable, for it offers many more options and becomes much more treacherous: triangles and scapulas appear when you least expect them, armlocks occur right after a sweep defense, and so on. There is a saying: "Never rest in the middle of anybody's guard; it can be very dangerous." The combination of sweeps and attacks is, again, almost infallible when done well.

• INVERTED ARMLOCK

Start in a closed guard and wait for the moment when your opponent starts to stand up.

Take advantage of the fact that he is off balance, and pull your legs out so as to force your opponent to seek support on the ground.

Put your foot on the ground on the same side of the arm you intend to attack, at the same time wrapping your arm around that of your opponent, as high as his elbow.

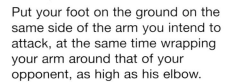

Grab your own collar with your hand and put the foot that was on the ground against your opponent's hips. Move your hips further out.

4

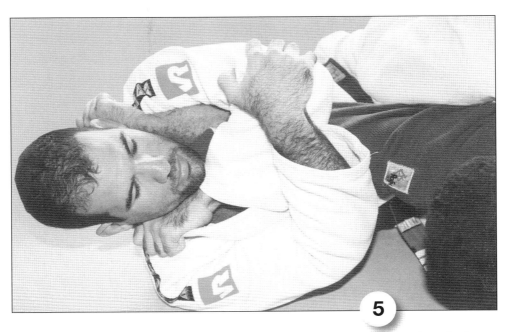

5

Press your elbow down with your other hand, and finish the inverted armlock. Always keep your foot against the opponent's hips, or he might propel his body weight upward and defend against the lock.

• ARMLOCK USING THE LAPEL

Start in a closed guard while your opponent is getting ready to stand up. With your hand on the same side as the arm that is supported on your chest, grab his lapel.

Pull the lapel to the outside of your opponent's body and, with your other hand, pull it very close to his triceps.

After gaining control, grab the sleeve of the arm being attacked, very close to your opponent's wrist so that he cannot free his arm.

Put your foot on the hip on the same side of the attacked arm, pulling as high up as the middle of your belly, and sliding your hips in a single move. Try to execute this movement when your opponent starts to raise himself.

Place the entire weight of your leg high on your opponent's back, keeping your hips well raised.

Pass the leg over his face and execute a guard armlock. Do not release your lapel grip until you have completed the movement.

• CHOKE USING THE COLLAR AND CROSSING THE ARM

Start in a closed guard while your opponent is getting ready to stand up. However, your opponent puts all his weight on his elbow, making an armlock difficult.

With your other hand, grab hold of his collar from behind his head and pull it from behind his neck.

Grab it again with the first hand that you used to grab the collar, but now with the palm of the hand facing up and the wrist held straight in choke position.

Slide your hip and execute the choke attack with the other hand over the opponent's shoulder. This may be enough to finish him, but in our example he defends himself by holding the hand against your shoulder, keeping you from pulling him to your chest for the choke.

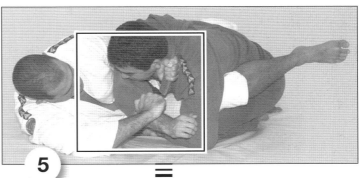

You must then grab the arm that is being held against you with the hand that was attempting the choke, pulling it diagonally. Press your shoulder forward, pulling the hand that is on his collar. You will be able to finish the choke with only one hand on the collar.

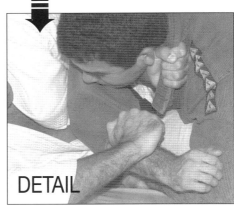

DETAIL

• CLOSED-GUARD FOOTLOCK

Start in a closed guard when your
opponent raises himself in order to
try to open your leg.

Putting your hand on the ground
as a support, raise your hip as high
as possible so that you can put the
opposite arm around the opponent's
leg.

Pull his foot and press your hips
down over the dominated leg,
which will make your opponent lose
balance.

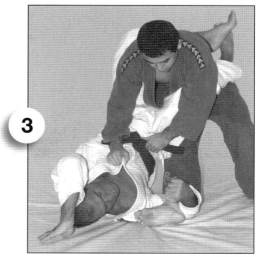

When he falls down, close a foot rear naked choke and finish the lock, preferably keeping your legs locked.

• CROSSED-HOOK LEGLOCK

Start the position as though you were going to sweep your opponent with crossed hooks.

Stretch the hooks and pull the opponent's leg, at the same time forcing him to put his hands on the ground as a support in order to maintain balance.

Put the foot on the same side of your opponent's hands under his armpit, pushing him away. Slide your hip so as to place your head very close to the foot that you are holding.

Pass the leg over your opponent's hips. Then take your foot off his armpit in order to lock the triangle. Hug his heel and carry the hip to finish in a leglock.

• CHOKE WITH ONE HAND INVERTED

Prepare the position when your opponent dominates your leg on the ground, and place the other leg on the inside, locking your hips.

When the opponent shifts his weight to pass the guard, hold back the shoulder and hip, so that when you are almost dominated you will still be able to slide your hip slightly to the outside.

Move your hand from the hip to the shoulder, and grab your opponent's collar with your other hand. Note that your hand must be positioned so that your thumb is facing down.

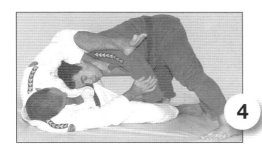

After grabbing a tight hold of your opponent's collar, put your leg on his back and press your elbow underneath.

Move your hips to the inside and grab the opponent's knee so as to keep him from rolling and undoing the attack. Keep pressing the elbow down and finish the choke.

• SCAPULA LOCK

This attack is
used when the
opponent is on
guard with his
elbow bent and
placed outside
the line of his
hips.

Put your foot
on the ground
on the opposite
side, moving
your hips
out. Push the
opponent's
wrist towards
his hips.

3

Pass your leg over the opponent's arm, completing a triangle, and put your arm around his waist. At the same time, thrust your foot out in order to alter your balance, and begin to sit down.

When sitting, put your leg back for better leverage, and keep your hand around the opponent's waist.

4

5

Lean your weight forward and down, finishing the shoulder-blade lock.

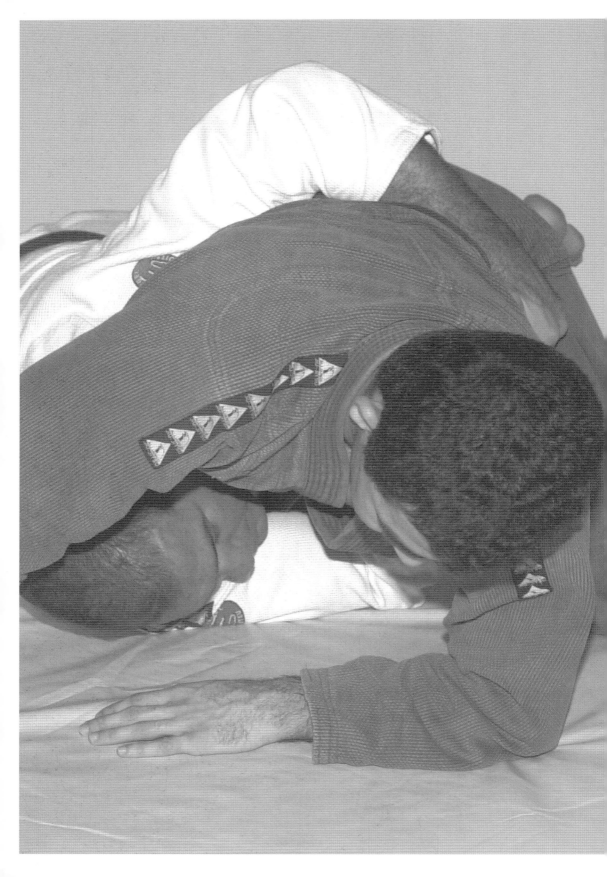

MOUNTED ESCAPES

It is essential that we understand Jiu-Jitsu as a defensive fighting style. According to this principle, the present subject is of utmost importance, since it deals with extricating oneself from difficult situations. In the first place, it is absolutely necessary to keep cool. But how to keep cool with a 240-lb. fighter mounted on you? The answer is: you must know the technique in order to remain calm. If the technique is perfect (and I know it is!), why should you be frightened? Once you understand this, you already have the advantage, for you will be able to consider how to create the best lever for this or that situation. After that, it is a piece of cake, for the techniques, as always, fit together perfectly, and your opponent cannot keep you dominated. This concept is extremely important, and it often defines the fight: if your opponent cannot win, he will ultimately lose.

• CLOCK DEFENSE AND GUARD

Your opponent
has you in
all-fours
domination.
Make sure to
keep your neck
protected in
order to avoid
the clock attack.

Raise the leg
on the side of
your opponent.
The hand on
his side must
try to grab his
attacking arm,
so as to relieve
choke pressure
as much as
possible.

Sit back, sliding
the kneeling
leg forward and
between your
opponent's
legs.

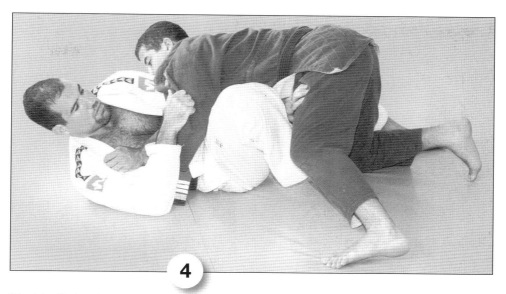

Start to lie back and move your hips to the inside, so as to face your opponent and recover guard.

Dominate his arm and move your hips out again, in order to lock the guard, and prepare to begin attacking.

• OUTSIDE REVERSAL

Start in side control. This time, your opponent tries to put his arm around your head in front of your face, which keeps you from using the previous technique, the inside reversal.

Create a bridge to the inside, trying to make room for an escape.

Quickly move back and turn outward, over the other shoulder.

Land on all fours. Put the hand that is on the same side as the opponent around his leg.

Pull his leg as in the previous technique, dominating him in side control.

• SOMERSAULT WITH HEAD HELD

Your opponent has you in side control, hugging your head. Pay attention to how you place your arms, because your elbow must always be under your opponent's hips.

Make a bridge, so as to make room for a hip escape. Make sure that the soles of your feet and one of your shoulders keep touching the ground.

Move the hand that was on the shoulder and put it over your opponent's shoulder and onto his belt.

Your opponent will try to move forward in order to retain control. Use his weight to your own advantage, and start making a bridge to the other side.

4

5

Raise your hips from the ground and roll your opponent over the shoulder that is still touching the ground.

6

Go into side control. Note the possibility of proceeding to attack the arm that remained over your shoulder.

• FENCING AND REAR MOVE

Your opponent has you in side control, hugging your head. Pay attention to how you place your arms, because your elbow must always be under your opponent's hips.

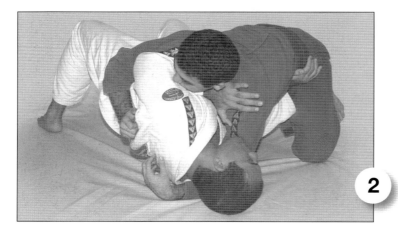

Make a bridge to the side where your opponent is located. Try to extend the arm on your opponent's hip, so as to make even more room. At the same time, slide your hip in order to escape.

There must be enough room for you to move your hand under your opponent's armpit.

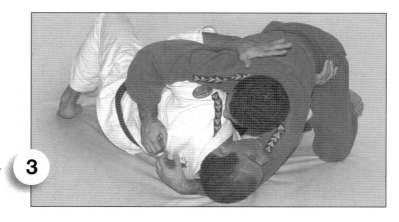

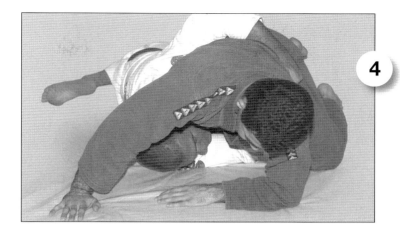

Move your hips down, so that your arm is under your opponent's arm, out of his reach, and then hug his back.

Get on all fours and then into rear attack position.

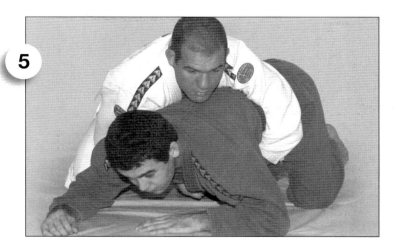

• FENCING AND SOMERSAULT

Start in the same position as in the previous techniques. Pay attention to the elbow under the hips and to the other hand that is resting on your opponent's shoulder. Be sure to keep your elbow close to his body.

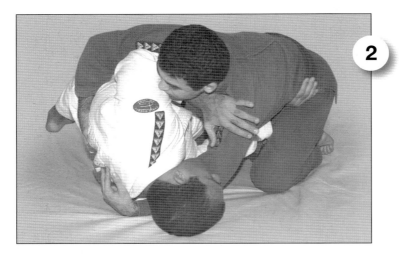

2 Make a bridge by holding his hip back and sliding your own hip backwards.

Move your hand under your opponent's armpit. **3**

4 Your opponent then embraces your arm and grabs your lapel, which keeps you from moving to the rear.

Turn your hip completely to the other side and push the opponent's hip with the hand that you had been using to restrain him. Roll him over your belly to the other side.

5

Assume side control.

6

• ESCAPE WITH HEAD UNDER ARMPIT

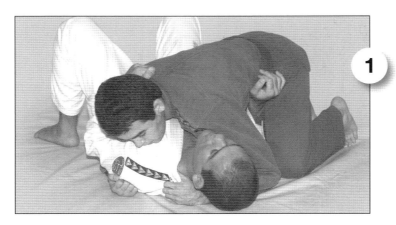

In control position, note that your arm is on the other side of the opponent's head.

1

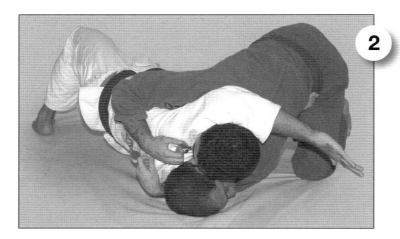

2 Make a bridge by extending your arm, as if you were going to touch the ground. Your biceps must move your opponent's head, so as to make him lose balance.

Keep your hand held against his hip with one arm stretched, and grab his triceps with your other hand. **3**

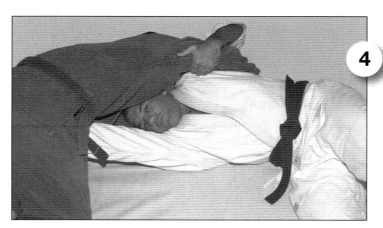

4 Start moving your hand to the outer side of your opponent's body.

5 Move your legs forward and take your head from under his body, placing it on his back.

Turn on your knees and assume a control position.

6

• ESCAPE WITH FOOT ON BICEPS AND CRUCIFIX

1

Your opponent has you in an inverted position. Keep your arms drawn up.

2 Push your opponent's chest up and draw your legs up, so that your knees fill the space between you and your opponent, and hold back his biceps with your shins.

Turn your hips down, but put one foot against your opponent's biceps. **3**

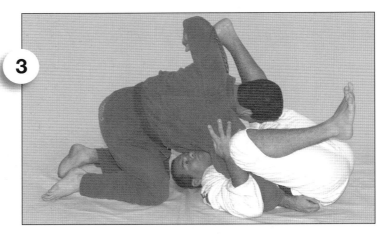

4 Put your other leg up from behind your opponent's arm, and then move it in front of the biceps that you had been restraining with your foot.

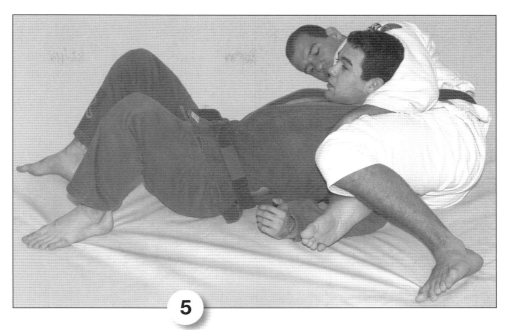

Pull back with the leg that you had put around the opponent's arm, and lock the crucifix.

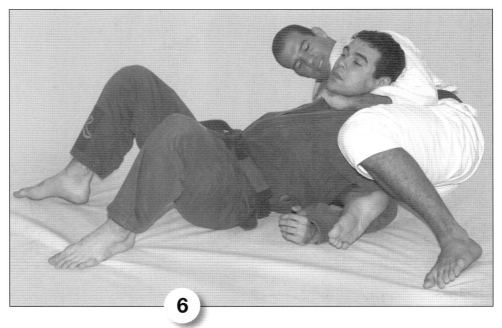

Put your hand on the opponent's collar and choke him.

THROWS

The standing part, though not as decisive in Jiu-Jitsu – where it is worth just two points, as it is in Judo – is very important from the aspect of personal defense. It is becoming more and more of a distinctive mark in competition Jiu-Jitsu, often allowing you to begin the fight in the upper position, which may be considered an advantage. Throws are clearly based on a lever principle, which the student must master. This principle teaches a great deal about balance, promoting a good stance, which is essential for any fighter. Many tend to look down on foot training, but I assure you it is just as important as any other part of Jiu-Jitsu.

• IPPON SEOI ON YOUR KNEES

Start in the basic grabbing position, with one hand on your opponent's lapel and the other on his arm.

Change the arm grab for a lapel grab on the same side, by going over your opponent's arm.

When your opponent projects his weight forward, go in by taking a diagonal step with the leg opposite the dominated lapel, and put your arm in under his armpit as if you were going to punch the ceiling.

4 Pull your opponent's collar and lapel, and kneel down between his legs.

Throw your opponent over your shoulder while looking towards the other side.

5

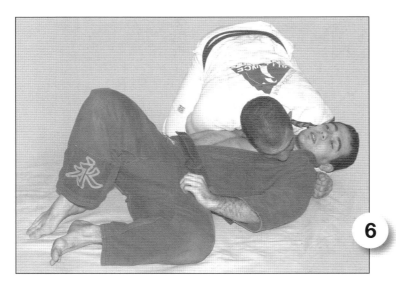

6 Assume side control.

• LEG GRAB WITH HEAD OUTSIDE

Project your body slightly forward, and then grab your opponent's kimono.

Determine which of your opponent's legs is closer to you, go in with your arm diagonally between his legs and, keeping your head on the outside, put that arm around the selected leg.

Hug your opponent's leg and pay attention to the grabbing details (palms must be close together, and the five fingers next to each other).

4 Pull the opponent's leg up and towards the middle of your legs by pressing one knee against the other.

Keep the foot that is between your opponent's legs on the ground, and execute a semicircle with the other, pressing your shoulder down and causing your opponent to lose his balance and fall down.

5

6 When you feel your opponent falling, do not project your body forward. Always keep your weight distributed between your legs to avoid a counterattack.

• LEG GRAB WITH DEFENSE

Start the position, and then grab your opponent's kimono.

Dominate the leg that is closer to you by kneeling down and hugging it.

Your opponent tries a leg defense consisting of extending his legs back and putting his hips over your shoulder.

4 Keep one hand on your opponent's leg and raise your leg on the same side. Put your other hand on the ground for support and extend your arm, so as to make more room under your opponent.

Move the knee that was on the ground under your opponent's hips and take a step towards the outside with your other leg. Your hand must pull the opponent's leg up at the same time, forcing him to put his hands on the ground. **5**

6 Grab his other leg with the hand that was on the ground, and pull it towards you.

Dominate from above by keeping your opponent's back on the ground.

• KATAGURUMA

Start in the basic grabbing position.

Change the grab over the arm, leaving the other hand free.

Pull the dominated lapel and take a diagonal step between your opponent's legs, while simultaneously going in with your hand in another diagonal move, to grab his leg. Your head must remain outside your opponent's body.

Take a big step forward with your rear leg, extending it so as to make a wedge on your opponent's foot. Lie back and throw him over your shoulder.

Continue the movement by taking one step in order to turn your opponent belly-down.

6 Finish in side control.

• TANI OTOSHI

Start in a basic grabbing position.   **1**

2 Switch the grab from one arm to the other, then change the collar grab in order to grab hold of your opponent's belt from over his shoulder.

3 Move sideways and extend the leg behind your opponent, sitting on your heels (be careful not to throw your body over your opponent's leg, as you may injure it). Put your head on his chest, pushing him down and then back.

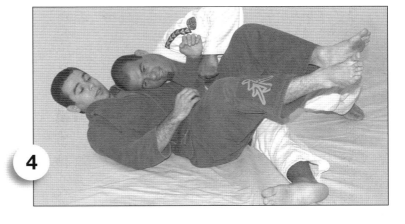

Throw your opponent down and keep your head over his chest.

4

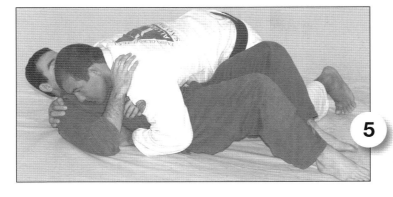

5 Turn around to face him and go into side control.

• TOMOE NAGUE

In the initial grab position, take one step between your opponent's legs with the leg of the same side as the hand that is holding his lapel.

Place the other foot as high as your opponent's belt and start to lie back, pulling his arm and lapel.

Lie back and start pushing the foot that is on his hip, at the same time pulling your opponent's arm and lapel, so as to propel his weight as far forward as possible.

Lift your opponent up with the foot
on his hips, and make a hook with
the other foot, just behind his knee
joint, in order to maintain balance.

Roll back with the help of your
opponent's weight, which naturally
pulls you up.

Complete the fall by assuming a mount position.

• OUCHI GARI

Starting from the initial grab position, take a step forward between your opponent's legs with the leg on the same side as the hand holding his collar.

Move the other foot forward and look over the hand holding your opponent's collar.

Put your chest close to your opponent's, make an inside hook with your leg, sliding your toes across the ground, and pull down his collar so as to cause him to lose balance towards the same side as the hooked leg.

Lean your weight forward, raising your leg and pushing the opponent's collar down. Keep looking at the collar.

4

Throw the opponent to the ground, and stand up to begin a guard pass.

5

• MOROTE SEOI NAGE

Start your movement with the
traditional collar grab.

1

2

Take one diagonal step and
simultaneously push down the elbow
of the arm whose hand is on your
opponent's collar. To do this, pull his
arm towards you to make him lose
his balance and lean forward.

Step back with the other foot, so as
to align it with the first one, and point
both feet forward, turning your back
to your opponent. Bend both legs so
as to place your hips under his waist.

3

Look to the side opposite the fall and turn your torso at the same time that you stretch your legs and propel your opponent forward, finishing the throw.

4

5

Finish the fall and prepare to execute an arm attack, or even a knee-on-stomach domination.

Fabio Duca Gurgel do Amaral

Eight-time World Champion Fabio Duca Gurgel do Amaral began practicing Jiu-Jitsu at the age of 13 and received his black belt at the age of 19. Along with his master, Romero Jacaré, he is the co-founder of the two-time World Champion Alliance Team with 40 academies around the world – from Venezuela to New York, from Finland to Germany. Gurgel continues to teach at his own academy in São Paulo and gives seminars throughout the world. He is president of the Professional League of Jiu-Jitsu.

"Fabio Gurgel to me is one of the best modern Jiu-Jitsu fighters of his time. He still competes and does very well at the masters division; he also represented Jiu-Jitsu against Wrestling in one of the best MMA matches of the 90s. He is my first black belt and a great friend. I am very grateful to God to have met him and have been able to touch his life."

Romero Jacaré